50 Truffle-Flavored Gourmet Meal Recipes for Home

By: Kelly Johnson

Table of Contents

- Truffle Risotto
- Truffle Macaroni and Cheese
- Truffle Mashed Potatoes
- Truffle Buttered Corn
- Truffle Scrambled Eggs
- Truffle Deviled Eggs
- Truffle Caesar Salad
- Truffle Pasta Carbonara
- Truffle Pizza
- Truffle Grilled Cheese Sandwich
- Truffle Potato Soup
- Truffle Crostini
- Truffle Garlic Bread
- Truffle Stuffed Mushrooms
- Truffle Bruschetta
- Truffle Beef Tenderloin
- Truffle Chicken Alfredo
- Truffle Lobster Linguine
- Truffle Salmon Fillet
- Truffle Goat Cheese Tart
- Truffle Wild Rice Pilaf
- Truffle Asparagus Risotto
- Truffle Roasted Brussels Sprouts
- Truffle Cauliflower Gratin
- Truffle Creamed Spinach
- Truffle Polenta Fries
- Truffle Tuna Tartare
- Truffle Crab Cakes
- Truffle Shrimp Scampi
- Truffle Stuffed Chicken Breast
- Truffle Quiche
- Truffle Gnocchi
- Truffle Beef Wellington
- Truffle Ratatouille
- Truffle Eggplant Parmesan

- Truffle Lamb Chops
- Truffle Paella
- Truffle Vegetable Stir-fry
- Truffle Beef Stroganoff
- Truffle Saffron Risotto
- Truffle Corn Chowder
- Truffle Potato Gratin
- Truffle Baked Brie
- Truffle Tomato Bruschetta
- Truffle Avocado Toast
- Truffle Caprese Salad
- Truffle Spinach and Artichoke Dip
- Truffle Pesto Pasta
- Truffle Chicken Piccata
- Truffle Chocolate Fondue

Truffle Risotto

Ingredients:

- 1 cup Arborio rice
- 4 cups vegetable or chicken broth
- 1/2 cup dry white wine
- 2 tablespoons unsalted butter
- 1 tablespoon olive oil
- 1 small onion, finely chopped
- 2 cloves garlic, minced
- 1/4 cup grated Parmesan cheese
- 2 tablespoons truffle oil
- Salt and pepper to taste
- Fresh parsley or chives, chopped, for garnish (optional)

Instructions:

In a saucepan, heat the vegetable or chicken broth over low heat. Keep it warm while you prepare the risotto.

In a separate large skillet or saucepan, heat the olive oil and 1 tablespoon of butter over medium heat.

Add the chopped onion to the skillet and cook until softened, about 3-4 minutes.

Add the minced garlic to the skillet and cook for an additional 1-2 minutes, until fragrant.

Add the Arborio rice to the skillet and cook, stirring constantly, for about 2 minutes until the rice is lightly toasted and coated in the oil.

Pour in the white wine and cook, stirring constantly, until it has been absorbed by the rice.

Begin adding the warm broth to the skillet, one ladleful at a time, stirring constantly and allowing each addition to be absorbed by the rice before adding more. Continue this process until the rice is creamy and cooked al dente, which should take about 18-20 minutes. You may not need to use all of the broth.

Once the risotto is cooked, remove it from the heat and stir in the grated Parmesan cheese and remaining tablespoon of butter until melted and incorporated.

Drizzle the truffle oil over the risotto and stir to combine. Season with salt and pepper to taste.

Serve the Truffle Risotto immediately, garnished with chopped fresh parsley or chives if desired.

Enjoy your luxurious and flavorful Truffle Risotto as a main course or side dish!

This Truffle Risotto is creamy, aromatic, and rich in flavor, making it a perfect dish for special occasions or a fancy dinner at home. Serve it alongside a crisp green salad or roasted vegetables for a complete meal. Feel free to customize the recipe by adding mushrooms, peas, or other ingredients to suit your taste preferences.

Truffle Macaroni and Cheese

Ingredients:

- 8 oz (about 2 cups) elbow macaroni or your favorite pasta shape
- 4 tablespoons unsalted butter
- 1/4 cup all-purpose flour
- 2 cups whole milk
- 1 cup heavy cream
- 2 cups shredded cheese (such as sharp cheddar, Gruyère, or a combination)
- 2 tablespoons truffle oil
- 1/4 cup grated Parmesan cheese
- Salt and pepper to taste
- Optional: 1/4 cup breadcrumbs for topping

Instructions:

Preheat your oven to 375°F (190°C). Grease a 9x13-inch baking dish with butter or cooking spray.

Cook the elbow macaroni or pasta according to the package instructions until al dente. Drain and set aside.

In a large saucepan, melt the butter over medium heat. Once melted, whisk in the flour to form a roux. Cook for 1-2 minutes, stirring constantly, until the roux is golden brown and fragrant.

Gradually pour in the whole milk and heavy cream, whisking constantly to prevent lumps from forming. Continue to cook, stirring frequently, until the sauce thickens and coats the back of a spoon, about 5-7 minutes.

Reduce the heat to low and gradually stir in the shredded cheese until melted and smooth, creating a creamy cheese sauce.

Stir in the truffle oil and grated Parmesan cheese until well combined. Season the sauce with salt and pepper to taste.

Add the cooked macaroni or pasta to the cheese sauce, stirring until evenly coated.

Pour the truffle macaroni and cheese mixture into the prepared baking dish, spreading it out evenly.

Optional: Sprinkle breadcrumbs evenly over the top of the macaroni and cheese for a crispy topping.

Bake the Truffle Macaroni and Cheese in the preheated oven for 20-25 minutes, or until the top is golden brown and bubbly.

Once done, remove the baking dish from the oven and let it cool for a few minutes before serving.

Serve the Truffle Macaroni and Cheese hot as a delicious and indulgent side dish or main course.

Enjoy your luxurious and creamy Truffle Macaroni and Cheese!

This Truffle Macaroni and Cheese is rich, creamy, and full of flavor, with the decadent aroma of truffle oil adding a gourmet touch to the classic comfort food. Serve it as a side dish at your next dinner party or enjoy it as a comforting meal on a cozy night in. Feel free to customize the recipe by adding crispy bacon, sautéed mushrooms, or chopped herbs for extra flavor and texture.

Truffle Mashed Potatoes

Ingredients:

- 2 lbs (about 4 large) Russet potatoes, peeled and cut into chunks
- 4 tablespoons unsalted butter
- 1/2 cup heavy cream
- 2 tablespoons truffle oil
- 2 cloves garlic, minced
- Salt and pepper to taste
- Chopped fresh chives or parsley for garnish (optional)

Instructions:

Place the peeled and chopped potatoes in a large pot and cover them with cold water. Add a generous pinch of salt to the water.
Bring the pot of water to a boil over high heat. Once boiling, reduce the heat to medium-low and let the potatoes simmer until they are fork-tender, about 15-20 minutes.
While the potatoes are cooking, in a small saucepan, melt the butter over medium heat. Add the minced garlic to the melted butter and cook for 1-2 minutes until fragrant, being careful not to let it brown.
Once the potatoes are cooked, drain them well and return them to the pot.
Mash the potatoes with a potato masher or fork until they reach your desired consistency.
Gradually pour the melted butter and garlic mixture, heavy cream, and truffle oil into the mashed potatoes, stirring until well combined and creamy. You may adjust the amount of cream and truffle oil to achieve the desired texture and flavor.
Season the Truffle Mashed Potatoes with salt and pepper to taste, and stir until evenly distributed.
Transfer the mashed potatoes to a serving dish and garnish with chopped fresh chives or parsley, if desired.
Serve the Truffle Mashed Potatoes hot as a luxurious and flavorful side dish.
Enjoy your decadent Truffle Mashed Potatoes alongside your favorite main course!

These Truffle Mashed Potatoes are creamy, aromatic, and rich in flavor, with the luxurious aroma of truffle oil adding a gourmet touch. They are the perfect accompaniment to roasted meats, grilled vegetables, or any holiday feast. Feel free to customize the recipe by adding grated Parmesan cheese, roasted garlic, or crispy bacon for extra flavor and texture.

Truffle Buttered Corn

Ingredients:

- 4 cups corn kernels (fresh, frozen, or canned)
- 2 tablespoons truffle butter
- 1 tablespoon olive oil
- 2 cloves garlic, minced
- Salt and pepper to taste
- Chopped fresh parsley or chives for garnish (optional)

Instructions:

If using fresh corn, shuck the corn and remove the kernels from the cob. If using frozen corn, thaw it according to the package instructions. If using canned corn, drain and rinse it.
In a large skillet or frying pan, heat the truffle butter and olive oil over medium heat until the butter is melted.
Add the minced garlic to the skillet and sauté for 1-2 minutes until fragrant, being careful not to let it brown.
Add the corn kernels to the skillet and toss to coat them evenly with the truffle butter and garlic mixture.
Cook the corn, stirring occasionally, for 5-7 minutes until heated through and slightly caramelized.
Season the Truffle Buttered Corn with salt and pepper to taste, and stir to combine.
Once the corn is cooked to your liking, remove the skillet from the heat.
Transfer the Truffle Buttered Corn to a serving dish and garnish with chopped fresh parsley or chives, if desired.
Serve the Truffle Buttered Corn hot as a decadent and flavorful side dish.
Enjoy your luxurious Truffle Buttered Corn alongside your favorite main course!

This Truffle Buttered Corn is rich, aromatic, and bursting with flavor, with the luxurious aroma of truffle butter adding a gourmet touch. It's the perfect accompaniment to grilled meats, seafood, or roasted vegetables, and it's sure to impress your guests at any dinner party or holiday feast. Feel free to customize the recipe by adding grated Parmesan cheese, chopped bacon, or red pepper flakes for extra flavor and texture.

Truffle Scrambled Eggs

Ingredients:

- 4 large eggs
- 2 tablespoons heavy cream
- 1 tablespoon truffle oil
- Salt and pepper to taste
- Chopped fresh chives or parsley for garnish (optional)

Instructions:

Crack the eggs into a mixing bowl and whisk them together with the heavy cream until well combined and slightly frothy. Season with salt and pepper to taste.
Heat a non-stick skillet over medium-low heat and add the truffle oil.
Once the truffle oil is heated, pour the beaten eggs into the skillet.
Let the eggs cook undisturbed for a few seconds until the edges start to set.
Using a spatula, gently push the cooked edges of the eggs toward the center of the skillet, allowing the uncooked eggs to flow to the edges.
Continue to gently stir and fold the eggs as they cook, until they are just set but still slightly creamy and moist.
Once the eggs reach your desired consistency, remove the skillet from the heat immediately to prevent overcooking.
Transfer the Truffle Scrambled Eggs to a serving plate or bowl.
Garnish with chopped fresh chives or parsley, if desired, for a pop of color and freshness.
Serve the Truffle Scrambled Eggs hot and enjoy their luxurious aroma and flavor!

These Truffle Scrambled Eggs are creamy, aromatic, and indulgent, with the delicate flavor of truffle oil elevating the humble scrambled eggs to gourmet heights. They make a delicious and elegant breakfast or brunch option, and they're sure to impress your family and guests. Feel free to customize the recipe by adding grated Parmesan cheese or chopped mushrooms for extra flavor and texture.

Truffle Deviled Eggs

Ingredients:

- 6 hard-boiled eggs, peeled and halved lengthwise
- 2 tablespoons mayonnaise
- 1 tablespoon Dijon mustard
- 1 tablespoon truffle oil
- 1 teaspoon white wine vinegar
- Salt and pepper to taste
- Chopped fresh chives or parsley for garnish (optional)

Instructions:

Carefully remove the yolks from the halved hard-boiled eggs and transfer them to a mixing bowl.

Mash the egg yolks with a fork until they are finely crumbled.

Add the mayonnaise, Dijon mustard, truffle oil, and white wine vinegar to the bowl with the mashed egg yolks.

Stir the ingredients together until smooth and well combined. If the mixture is too thick, you can add a little more mayonnaise or a splash of water to reach your desired consistency.

Season the filling with salt and pepper to taste, adjusting the seasoning as needed.

Spoon or pipe the truffle deviled egg filling into the hollowed-out egg white halves, dividing it evenly among them.

Garnish each Truffle Deviled Egg with chopped fresh chives or parsley, if desired, for a pop of color and freshness.

Serve the Truffle Deviled Eggs immediately as an elegant and flavorful appetizer. Enjoy the luxurious aroma and flavor of these Truffle Deviled Eggs!

These Truffle Deviled Eggs are creamy, indulgent, and packed with the delicate flavor of truffle oil, making them a sophisticated twist on a classic favorite. They're perfect for serving at cocktail parties, brunches, or any special occasion where you want to impress your guests with a gourmet appetizer. Feel free to customize the recipe by adding minced shallots, grated Parmesan cheese, or crispy bacon for extra flavor and texture.

Truffle Caesar Salad

Ingredients:

For the Salad:

- 1 head of romaine lettuce, washed and chopped
- 1/2 cup croutons (store-bought or homemade)
- 1/4 cup grated Parmesan cheese

For the Dressing:

- 1/4 cup mayonnaise
- 2 tablespoons lemon juice
- 1 tablespoon Dijon mustard
- 1 tablespoon Worcestershire sauce
- 2 cloves garlic, minced
- 2 anchovy fillets, minced (optional)
- 1 tablespoon truffle oil
- Salt and pepper to taste

Instructions:

In a large salad bowl, combine the chopped romaine lettuce, croutons, and grated Parmesan cheese. Toss to combine.

In a small bowl, whisk together the mayonnaise, lemon juice, Dijon mustard, Worcestershire sauce, minced garlic, and minced anchovy fillets (if using) until well combined.

Gradually drizzle in the truffle oil while whisking constantly until the dressing is smooth and creamy.

Taste the dressing and adjust the seasoning with salt and pepper as needed.

Pour the truffle Caesar dressing over the salad and toss until the lettuce is evenly coated with the dressing.

Serve the Truffle Caesar Salad immediately as a delicious and luxurious appetizer or side dish.

Enjoy the rich and flavorful taste of this Truffle Caesar Salad!

This Truffle Caesar Salad is creamy, aromatic, and packed with flavor, thanks to the addition of truffle oil to the classic Caesar dressing. It's the perfect starter or accompaniment to any meal, and it's sure to impress your guests with its gourmet flair. Feel free to customize the salad by adding grilled chicken, shrimp, or sliced avocado for extra protein and texture.

Truffle Pasta Carbonara

Ingredients:

- 12 oz (340g) spaghetti or fettuccine
- 4 large eggs
- 1 cup grated Parmesan cheese, plus extra for serving
- 8 slices of bacon or pancetta, diced
- 2 cloves garlic, minced
- 2 tablespoons truffle oil
- Salt and black pepper to taste
- Chopped fresh parsley for garnish (optional)

Instructions:

Cook the pasta according to the package instructions until al dente. Reserve 1 cup of pasta cooking water, then drain the pasta and set aside.
In a mixing bowl, whisk together the eggs and grated Parmesan cheese until well combined. Set aside.
In a large skillet, cook the diced bacon or pancetta over medium heat until crispy. Remove the cooked bacon from the skillet and drain on paper towels. Discard excess grease, leaving about 1 tablespoon in the skillet.
In the same skillet, add the minced garlic and cook for about 1 minute until fragrant.
Reduce the heat to low and return the cooked bacon to the skillet. Add the cooked pasta to the skillet and toss to combine with the bacon and garlic.
Remove the skillet from the heat and quickly pour the egg and cheese mixture over the pasta, tossing continuously to coat the pasta evenly. The heat from the pasta will cook the eggs and create a creamy sauce.
Drizzle the truffle oil over the pasta and toss to combine.
If the sauce seems too thick, gradually add some of the reserved pasta cooking water until you reach your desired consistency.
Season the Truffle Pasta Carbonara with salt and black pepper to taste.
Serve the pasta immediately, garnished with extra grated Parmesan cheese and chopped fresh parsley if desired.
Enjoy your luxurious Truffle Pasta Carbonara!

This Truffle Pasta Carbonara is creamy, rich, and packed with flavor, with the addition of truffle oil adding a gourmet touch to the classic dish. Serve it as a main course for a special dinner or as a decadent indulgence any day of the week. Feel free to customize the recipe by adding mushrooms, peas, or spinach for extra flavor and texture.

Truffle Pizza

Ingredients:

- 1 pizza dough (store-bought or homemade)
- 2 tablespoons truffle oil
- 1/2 cup pizza sauce
- 1 1/2 cups shredded mozzarella cheese
- 1/4 cup grated Parmesan cheese
- 1/4 cup sliced mushrooms
- 2 tablespoons chopped fresh parsley
- Salt and pepper to taste

Instructions:

Preheat your oven to the highest temperature setting (usually around 450-500°F or 230-260°C). If you have a pizza stone, place it in the oven to preheat as well.
Roll out the pizza dough on a lightly floured surface to your desired thickness.
Transfer the dough to a pizza peel or parchment paper-lined baking sheet.
Drizzle the truffle oil evenly over the surface of the pizza dough, leaving a small border around the edges.
Spread the pizza sauce over the truffle oil, covering the entire surface of the dough.
Sprinkle the shredded mozzarella cheese evenly over the sauce.
Scatter the sliced mushrooms over the cheese.
Season the pizza with salt and pepper to taste.
Transfer the pizza to the preheated oven, either directly onto the pizza stone or onto the baking sheet if using.
Bake the pizza for 10-12 minutes, or until the crust is golden brown and the cheese is melted and bubbly.
Once done, remove the pizza from the oven and sprinkle the grated Parmesan cheese and chopped fresh parsley over the top.
Slice the Truffle Pizza into wedges and serve hot.
Enjoy your delicious and gourmet Truffle Pizza!

This Truffle Pizza is sure to impress with its rich and aromatic flavor. You can customize it by adding toppings like prosciutto, arugula, or caramelized onions for extra depth of flavor. Serve it as an appetizer, main course, or even as a gourmet snack for a special occasion.

Truffle Grilled Cheese Sandwich

Ingredients:

- 4 slices of bread (your choice of bread, but a sturdy bread like sourdough works well)
- 4 ounces (about 1 cup) shredded cheese (such as Gruyère, cheddar, or fontina)
- 2 tablespoons truffle butter or truffle oil
- 1 tablespoon mayonnaise
- Optional: sliced mushrooms, caramelized onions, or cooked bacon for extra flavor

Instructions:

    Preheat a skillet or griddle over medium heat.
    Spread truffle butter on one side of each slice of bread.
    Place two slices of bread butter side down on the skillet or griddle.
    Sprinkle shredded cheese evenly over the bread slices.
    If using any additional toppings like sliced mushrooms, caramelized onions, or cooked bacon, add them on top of the cheese.
    Place the remaining slices of bread on top, butter side up.
    Cook the sandwiches for 3-4 minutes on each side, or until the bread is golden brown and the cheese is melted.
    While the sandwiches are cooking, spread mayonnaise on the top slice of each sandwich. This will help the bread develop a golden crust and adds extra flavor.
    Once the sandwiches are done, remove them from the skillet or griddle and let them cool for a minute.
    Slice the Truffle Grilled Cheese Sandwiches diagonally and serve hot.
    Enjoy your indulgent and flavorful Truffle Grilled Cheese Sandwiches!

This Truffle Grilled Cheese Sandwich is rich, creamy, and packed with the luxurious aroma of truffle butter. It's perfect for a cozy lunch or dinner, and you can customize it with your favorite cheese and additional toppings for extra flavor. Serve it alongside a bowl of tomato soup for the ultimate comfort food experience.

Truffle Potato Soup

Ingredients:

- 4 large potatoes, peeled and diced
- 1 onion, chopped
- 2 cloves garlic, minced
- 4 cups vegetable or chicken broth
- 1 cup heavy cream
- 2 tablespoons truffle oil
- Salt and pepper to taste
- Chopped fresh chives or parsley for garnish (optional)

Instructions:

In a large pot or Dutch oven, heat a drizzle of olive oil over medium heat. Add the chopped onion and minced garlic, and sauté until softened and fragrant, about 3-4 minutes.
Add the diced potatoes to the pot, and pour in the vegetable or chicken broth. Bring the mixture to a boil, then reduce the heat to low and let it simmer until the potatoes are fork-tender, about 15-20 minutes.
Once the potatoes are cooked, use an immersion blender to blend the soup until smooth and creamy. Alternatively, you can transfer the soup in batches to a blender and blend until smooth, then return it to the pot.
Stir in the heavy cream and truffle oil until well combined. Season the soup with salt and pepper to taste.
Continue to simmer the soup for another 5-10 minutes to allow the flavors to meld together.
Once done, remove the pot from the heat.
Ladle the Truffle Potato Soup into bowls and garnish with chopped fresh chives or parsley, if desired.
Serve the soup hot, and enjoy its rich and comforting flavor!

This Truffle Potato Soup is creamy, aromatic, and perfect for warming up on a chilly day. The addition of truffle oil adds a luxurious touch, elevating the humble potato soup to a gourmet dish. Serve it as a starter or pair it with crusty bread for a satisfying meal. Feel free to customize the recipe by adding crispy bacon, grated Parmesan cheese, or sautéed mushrooms for extra flavor and texture.

Truffle Crostini

Ingredients:

- Baguette or French bread, sliced into 1/2-inch thick slices
- 2 tablespoons truffle oil
- 4 ounces (about 1 cup) ricotta cheese
- 2 tablespoons chopped fresh chives
- Salt and pepper to taste
- Optional: shaved Parmesan cheese or grated Pecorino Romano cheese for topping
- Optional garnish: additional chopped fresh chives or parsley

Instructions:

Preheat your oven to 375°F (190°C).
Arrange the baguette or French bread slices on a baking sheet in a single layer.
Brush the bread slices lightly with truffle oil on both sides.
Place the baking sheet in the preheated oven and bake the bread slices for about 8-10 minutes, or until they are lightly golden and crispy. Keep an eye on them to prevent burning.
While the bread is baking, in a small bowl, mix the ricotta cheese with chopped fresh chives. Season with salt and pepper to taste.
Once the bread slices are toasted, remove them from the oven and let them cool slightly.
Spread a dollop of the ricotta mixture onto each crostini.
If desired, top each crostini with a few shavings of Parmesan cheese or grated Pecorino Romano cheese for extra flavor.
Garnish the Truffle Crostini with additional chopped fresh chives or parsley, if desired.
Serve the crostini immediately as a delicious and elegant appetizer.
Enjoy the rich and luxurious flavor of these Truffle Crostini!

These Truffle Crostini are perfect for entertaining guests or enjoying as a special treat at home. They are easy to make yet impressive in presentation, making them a great choice for cocktail parties, holiday gatherings, or any occasion where you want to impress your guests. Feel free to customize the recipe by adding other toppings such as sliced prosciutto, roasted mushrooms, or sun-dried tomatoes for additional flavor and texture.

Truffle Garlic Bread

Ingredients:

- 1 baguette or Italian bread loaf
- 4 tablespoons unsalted butter, softened
- 2 cloves garlic, minced
- 1 tablespoon truffle oil
- 2 tablespoons chopped fresh parsley (optional)
- Salt and pepper to taste
- Grated Parmesan cheese (optional)

Instructions:

Preheat your oven to 375°F (190°C).
Slice the baguette or Italian bread loaf lengthwise, creating two halves.
In a small bowl, combine the softened butter, minced garlic, truffle oil, chopped fresh parsley (if using), salt, and pepper. Mix until well combined.
Spread the truffle garlic butter mixture evenly over the cut sides of the bread halves.
If desired, sprinkle grated Parmesan cheese over the top of the garlic butter mixture.
Place the bread halves on a baking sheet, cut side up.
Bake in the preheated oven for 10-12 minutes, or until the edges are golden brown and the butter is melted and bubbly.
Once done, remove the truffle garlic bread from the oven and let it cool slightly.
Slice the bread into individual portions and serve warm.
Enjoy the rich and aromatic flavor of this truffle garlic bread as a delightful appetizer or side dish!

This truffle garlic bread is perfect for serving alongside pasta, soups, salads, or as a tasty snack on its own. The combination of garlic, butter, and truffle oil creates a wonderfully indulgent flavor that is sure to impress your family and guests. Feel free to customize the recipe by adding different herbs, cheeses, or spices to suit your taste preferences.

Truffle Stuffed Mushrooms

Ingredients:

- 12 large button mushrooms
- 1 tablespoon olive oil
- 2 cloves garlic, minced
- 1/4 cup finely chopped onion
- 1/4 cup breadcrumbs
- 2 tablespoons grated Parmesan cheese
- 1 tablespoon chopped fresh parsley
- 1 tablespoon truffle oil
- Salt and pepper to taste
- Optional: additional grated Parmesan cheese for topping

Instructions:

Preheat your oven to 375°F (190°C). Line a baking sheet with parchment paper or lightly grease it with olive oil.
Remove the stems from the mushrooms and finely chop them. Set the mushroom caps aside.
In a skillet, heat the olive oil over medium heat. Add the minced garlic and chopped onion, and sauté until softened, about 2-3 minutes.
Add the chopped mushroom stems to the skillet and cook for an additional 3-4 minutes, until they release their moisture and start to brown.
Remove the skillet from the heat and transfer the cooked mushroom mixture to a mixing bowl.
To the bowl, add the breadcrumbs, grated Parmesan cheese, chopped fresh parsley, truffle oil, salt, and pepper. Mix until well combined.
Using a spoon, fill each mushroom cap with the stuffing mixture, pressing gently to pack it in.
Place the stuffed mushrooms on the prepared baking sheet.
If desired, sprinkle additional grated Parmesan cheese over the top of each stuffed mushroom.
Bake in the preheated oven for 15-20 minutes, or until the mushrooms are tender and the filling is golden brown and crispy.
Once done, remove the truffle stuffed mushrooms from the oven and let them cool slightly before serving.
Serve the stuffed mushrooms warm as a delicious appetizer or side dish.

Enjoy the rich and flavorful taste of these truffle stuffed mushrooms!

These truffle stuffed mushrooms are perfect for entertaining guests or enjoying as a special treat at home. They are easy to make and bursting with delicious flavor, making them a hit at any party or gathering. Feel free to customize the recipe by adding chopped bacon, spinach, or other herbs and cheeses to the stuffing mixture for extra flavor and texture.

Truffle Bruschetta

Ingredients:

- 1 baguette, sliced into 1/2-inch thick slices
- 2 tablespoons truffle oil
- 2 cloves garlic, peeled and halved
- 2 large tomatoes, diced
- 1/4 cup fresh basil leaves, chopped
- 1 tablespoon balsamic vinegar
- Salt and pepper to taste
- Optional: grated Parmesan cheese for topping

Instructions:

Preheat your oven to 375°F (190°C).
Place the baguette slices on a baking sheet in a single layer.
Drizzle the truffle oil evenly over the baguette slices.
Rub the cut sides of the garlic cloves over the surface of each baguette slice to infuse them with garlic flavor.
Place the baking sheet in the preheated oven and bake the baguette slices for about 8-10 minutes, or until they are lightly golden and crispy. Keep an eye on them to prevent burning.
While the baguette slices are baking, in a mixing bowl, combine the diced tomatoes, chopped fresh basil, and balsamic vinegar. Season with salt and pepper to taste.
Once the baguette slices are toasted, remove them from the oven and let them cool slightly.
Spoon the tomato and basil mixture evenly onto each baguette slice.
If desired, sprinkle grated Parmesan cheese over the top of each bruschetta.
Serve the truffle bruschetta immediately as a delicious and elegant appetizer.
Enjoy the rich and flavorful taste of these truffle bruschetta!

This truffle bruschetta is perfect for entertaining guests or enjoying as a special treat at home. It's easy to make and bursting with delicious flavors, making it a hit at any party or gathering. Feel free to customize the recipe by adding other toppings such as sliced olives, roasted red peppers, or chopped onions for extra flavor and texture.

Truffle Beef Tenderloin

Ingredients:

- 1 whole beef tenderloin, trimmed (about 3-4 pounds)
- 2 tablespoons truffle oil
- 4 cloves garlic, minced
- 2 tablespoons chopped fresh thyme
- Salt and pepper to taste
- Optional: truffle butter or truffle salt for extra flavor

Instructions:

Preheat your oven to 425°F (220°C).
In a small bowl, mix together the truffle oil, minced garlic, and chopped fresh thyme to create a marinade.
Place the beef tenderloin in a roasting pan or baking dish. Pat the tenderloin dry with paper towels.
Rub the truffle oil mixture evenly over the surface of the beef tenderloin, coating it thoroughly. Make sure to massage the marinade into all sides of the meat.
Season the beef tenderloin generously with salt and pepper, to taste.
If desired, you can also add a pat of truffle butter on top of the beef tenderloin for extra richness and flavor. Alternatively, you can sprinkle truffle salt over the meat for a more intense truffle flavor.
Transfer the beef tenderloin to the preheated oven and roast for about 20-25 minutes per pound for medium-rare, or until a meat thermometer inserted into the thickest part of the meat registers 135°F (57°C).
Once the beef tenderloin reaches the desired level of doneness, remove it from the oven and let it rest for about 10 minutes before slicing.
Slice the Truffle Beef Tenderloin into thick slices and serve hot.
Enjoy the rich and flavorful taste of this Truffle Beef Tenderloin!

This Truffle Beef Tenderloin is tender, juicy, and packed with the luxurious aroma of truffle oil and garlic. It's perfect for serving as the centerpiece of a special meal or as part of a gourmet dinner spread. Pair it with your favorite side dishes such as roasted vegetables, mashed potatoes, or a green salad for a complete and delicious meal.

Truffle Chicken Alfredo

Ingredients:

- 8 ounces fettuccine pasta
- 2 boneless, skinless chicken breasts, cut into bite-sized pieces
- 2 tablespoons truffle oil
- 4 cloves garlic, minced
- 1 cup heavy cream
- 1/2 cup grated Parmesan cheese
- Salt and pepper to taste
- Chopped fresh parsley for garnish (optional)

Instructions:

Cook the fettuccine pasta according to the package instructions until al dente. Drain and set aside.

In a large skillet, heat 1 tablespoon of truffle oil over medium-high heat. Add the diced chicken pieces to the skillet and season with salt and pepper to taste. Cook until the chicken is golden brown and cooked through, about 5-6 minutes.

Remove the cooked chicken from the skillet and set aside.

In the same skillet, add the remaining tablespoon of truffle oil and minced garlic. Cook for about 1 minute, or until the garlic is fragrant but not browned.

Reduce the heat to medium-low and pour the heavy cream into the skillet. Stir to combine with the garlic and truffle oil.

Add the grated Parmesan cheese to the skillet and stir until the cheese is melted and the sauce is smooth and creamy.

Return the cooked chicken to the skillet and toss to coat it evenly with the sauce. Cook for an additional 2-3 minutes, or until the chicken is heated through.

Taste the sauce and adjust the seasoning with salt and pepper as needed.

Add the cooked fettuccine pasta to the skillet and toss to coat it evenly with the sauce.

Once everything is well combined and heated through, remove the skillet from the heat.

Serve the Truffle Chicken Alfredo hot, garnished with chopped fresh parsley if desired.

Enjoy the rich and luxurious flavor of this Truffle Chicken Alfredo!

This Truffle Chicken Alfredo is creamy, aromatic, and packed with flavor, thanks to the addition of truffle oil and Parmesan cheese. It's perfect for a cozy dinner at home or for entertaining guests on special occasions. Serve it with a side salad and garlic bread for a complete and delicious meal.

Truffle Lobster Linguine

Ingredients:

- 8 ounces linguine pasta
- 2 lobster tails, thawed if frozen
- 2 tablespoons truffle oil
- 4 cloves garlic, minced
- 1/2 cup dry white wine
- 1 cup heavy cream
- 1/4 cup grated Parmesan cheese
- Salt and pepper to taste
- Chopped fresh parsley for garnish (optional)

Instructions:

Cook the linguine pasta according to the package instructions until al dente. Drain and set aside.

While the pasta is cooking, prepare the lobster tails. Using kitchen shears, carefully cut along the top of each lobster tail shell to expose the meat. Gently remove the meat from the shells and cut it into bite-sized pieces.

In a large skillet, heat the truffle oil over medium heat. Add the minced garlic and cook for about 1 minute, or until fragrant.

Add the lobster pieces to the skillet and cook for 2-3 minutes, stirring occasionally, until they start to turn pink and are almost cooked through.

Pour in the white wine and bring to a simmer. Let it cook for another 2-3 minutes to reduce slightly.

Reduce the heat to medium-low and pour the heavy cream into the skillet. Stir to combine with the lobster and garlic.

Add the grated Parmesan cheese to the skillet and stir until the cheese is melted and the sauce is smooth and creamy.

Season the sauce with salt and pepper to taste.

Add the cooked linguine pasta to the skillet and toss to coat it evenly with the sauce and lobster pieces.

Once everything is well combined and heated through, remove the skillet from the heat.

Serve the Truffle Lobster Linguine hot, garnished with chopped fresh parsley if desired.

Enjoy the rich and indulgent flavor of this Truffle Lobster Linguine!

This Truffle Lobster Linguine is creamy, aromatic, and packed with flavor, thanks to the addition of truffle oil and Parmesan cheese. It's sure to impress your family and guests with its gourmet flair. Serve it with a glass of white wine and some crusty bread for a truly decadent meal.

Truffle Salmon Fillet

Ingredients:

- 4 salmon fillets, skin-on or skinless, about 6 ounces each
- 2 tablespoons truffle oil
- 2 cloves garlic, minced
- 2 tablespoons chopped fresh parsley
- Salt and pepper to taste
- Lemon wedges for serving

Instructions:

Preheat your oven to 400°F (200°C). Line a baking sheet with parchment paper or lightly grease it with olive oil.
Pat the salmon fillets dry with paper towels and place them on the prepared baking sheet.
In a small bowl, mix together the truffle oil, minced garlic, chopped fresh parsley, salt, and pepper.
Brush the truffle oil mixture evenly over the surface of each salmon fillet, coating them thoroughly.
Place the baking sheet in the preheated oven and bake the salmon fillets for about 12-15 minutes, or until they are cooked through and flake easily with a fork.
Once done, remove the Truffle Salmon Fillets from the oven and let them rest for a few minutes before serving.
Serve the salmon fillets hot, garnished with lemon wedges.
Enjoy the rich and flavorful taste of this Truffle Salmon Fillet!

This Truffle Salmon Fillet is tender, moist, and packed with the luxurious aroma of truffle oil and garlic. It's perfect for a special dinner at home or for entertaining guests on special occasions. Serve it with your favorite side dishes such as roasted vegetables, mashed potatoes, or a fresh salad for a complete and delicious meal.

Truffle Goat Cheese Tart

Ingredients:

For the Tart Crust:

- 1 1/4 cups all-purpose flour
- 1/2 teaspoon salt
- 1/2 cup unsalted butter, cold and cut into small cubes
- 2-3 tablespoons ice water

For the Filling:

- 8 ounces goat cheese, softened
- 1/4 cup heavy cream
- 2 tablespoons truffle oil
- 2 cloves garlic, minced
- Salt and pepper to taste
- 2 tablespoons chopped fresh chives for garnish

Instructions:

Preheat your oven to 375°F (190°C).
In a food processor, combine the all-purpose flour and salt. Add the cold butter cubes and pulse until the mixture resembles coarse crumbs.
Gradually add the ice water, 1 tablespoon at a time, and pulse until the dough comes together and forms a ball.
Transfer the dough to a lightly floured surface and roll it out into a circle large enough to fit your tart pan.
Carefully transfer the rolled-out dough to a 9-inch tart pan with a removable bottom. Press the dough into the bottom and up the sides of the pan. Trim off any excess dough.
Prick the bottom of the tart crust with a fork and place the tart pan in the refrigerator to chill for about 15 minutes.
Once chilled, line the tart crust with parchment paper and fill it with pie weights or dried beans. Blind bake the tart crust in the preheated oven for 15 minutes.

Remove the parchment paper and pie weights, and bake the tart crust for an additional 5-7 minutes, or until it is golden brown and crisp. Remove from the oven and let it cool slightly.

In a mixing bowl, combine the softened goat cheese, heavy cream, truffle oil, minced garlic, salt, and pepper. Mix until smooth and creamy.

Spread the goat cheese mixture evenly into the cooled tart crust.

Return the tart to the oven and bake for another 10-12 minutes, or until the filling is set.

Once done, remove the Truffle Goat Cheese Tart from the oven and let it cool slightly.

Garnish with chopped fresh chives before serving.

Slice the tart into wedges and serve warm or at room temperature.

Enjoy the rich and luxurious flavor of this Truffle Goat Cheese Tart!

This Truffle Goat Cheese Tart is perfect for serving as an appetizer or as part of a brunch spread. It's creamy, savory, and packed with the irresistible aroma of truffles. Serve it alongside a crisp green salad or roasted vegetables for a delicious and elegant meal.

Truffle Wild Rice Pilaf

Ingredients:

- 1 cup wild rice
- 2 1/2 cups vegetable or chicken broth
- 2 tablespoons truffle oil
- 1 small onion, finely chopped
- 2 cloves garlic, minced
- 1/4 cup chopped celery
- 1/4 cup chopped carrots
- 1/4 cup chopped mushrooms
- Salt and pepper to taste
- Chopped fresh parsley for garnish

Instructions:

Rinse the wild rice under cold water in a fine-mesh sieve until the water runs clear.

In a medium saucepan, bring the vegetable or chicken broth to a boil. Add the rinsed wild rice to the boiling broth.

Reduce the heat to low, cover the saucepan, and simmer the rice for about 45-50 minutes, or until the rice is tender and has absorbed most of the liquid. Remove from heat and let it sit, covered, for 5-10 minutes.

While the wild rice is cooking, heat the truffle oil in a large skillet over medium heat. Add the chopped onion, garlic, celery, carrots, and mushrooms to the skillet. Cook, stirring occasionally, until the vegetables are softened, about 5-7 minutes.

Once the wild rice is cooked, fluff it with a fork and transfer it to the skillet with the cooked vegetables.

Stir the rice and vegetables together until well combined. Season with salt and pepper to taste.

Continue to cook the Truffle Wild Rice Pilaf for another 2-3 minutes, stirring occasionally, to allow the flavors to meld together.

Once done, remove the skillet from the heat and transfer the pilaf to a serving dish.

Garnish the Truffle Wild Rice Pilaf with chopped fresh parsley before serving. Enjoy this delicious and aromatic side dish alongside your favorite main course!

This Truffle Wild Rice Pilaf is perfect for serving alongside roasted meats, poultry, or seafood. It's a flavorful and elegant addition to any meal, and the luxurious aroma of truffles adds a special touch to the dish. Feel free to customize the recipe by adding other vegetables or herbs according to your taste preferences.

Truffle Asparagus Risotto

Ingredients:

- 1 lb (450g) asparagus, trimmed and cut into bite-sized pieces
- 1 cup Arborio rice
- 4 cups vegetable or chicken broth
- 1 small onion, finely chopped
- 2 cloves garlic, minced
- 1/2 cup dry white wine
- 2 tablespoons truffle oil
- 1/2 cup grated Parmesan cheese
- Salt and pepper to taste
- Chopped fresh parsley for garnish

Instructions:

In a medium saucepan, bring the vegetable or chicken broth to a simmer over low heat. Keep the broth warm while you prepare the risotto.

In a large skillet or saucepan, heat 1 tablespoon of truffle oil over medium heat. Add the chopped onion and minced garlic, and cook until softened, about 2-3 minutes.

Add the Arborio rice to the skillet and cook, stirring constantly, for 1-2 minutes, until the rice is lightly toasted and coated with oil.

Pour in the white wine and cook, stirring, until the wine is absorbed by the rice. Begin adding the warm broth to the rice mixture, one ladleful at a time, stirring constantly and allowing each addition of broth to be absorbed before adding more. Continue this process until the rice is creamy and tender, but still slightly firm to the bite (al dente). This will take about 20-25 minutes.

While the risotto is cooking, heat the remaining tablespoon of truffle oil in a separate skillet over medium heat. Add the asparagus pieces and sauté until they are tender-crisp, about 5-7 minutes. Season with salt and pepper to taste.

Once the risotto is cooked to your desired consistency, stir in the grated Parmesan cheese until it is melted and well incorporated into the risotto.

Gently fold in the sautéed asparagus into the risotto, reserving a few pieces for garnish if desired. Season with additional salt and pepper to taste, if needed.

Remove the risotto from heat and let it rest for a minute or two.

Serve the Truffle Asparagus Risotto hot, garnished with chopped fresh parsley and additional asparagus pieces if desired.
Enjoy the creamy and flavorful Truffle Asparagus Risotto as a delicious main dish or side!

This Truffle Asparagus Risotto is creamy, savory, and packed with the luxurious aroma of truffles. It's perfect for a cozy dinner at home or for entertaining guests on special occasions. Serve it alongside a crisp green salad and a glass of white wine for a complete and delicious meal.

Truffle Roasted Brussels Sprouts

Ingredients:

- 1 lb (450g) Brussels sprouts, trimmed and halved
- 2 tablespoons olive oil
- 1 tablespoon truffle oil
- 2 cloves garlic, minced
- Salt and pepper to taste
- Grated Parmesan cheese (optional)
- Chopped fresh parsley for garnish (optional)

Instructions:

Preheat your oven to 400°F (200°C).
In a large mixing bowl, toss the halved Brussels sprouts with olive oil, truffle oil, minced garlic, salt, and pepper until they are evenly coated.
Spread the Brussels sprouts out in a single layer on a baking sheet lined with parchment paper or aluminum foil.
Roast the Brussels sprouts in the preheated oven for 20-25 minutes, or until they are golden brown and crispy on the outside, and tender on the inside. Stir them halfway through the cooking time to ensure even roasting.
Once the Brussels sprouts are done roasting, remove them from the oven and transfer them to a serving dish.
If desired, sprinkle grated Parmesan cheese over the roasted Brussels sprouts while they are still hot. The residual heat will melt the cheese.
Garnish the Truffle Roasted Brussels Sprouts with chopped fresh parsley for a pop of color and freshness.
Serve the roasted Brussels sprouts hot as a delicious side dish or appetizer.
Enjoy the rich and flavorful taste of these Truffle Roasted Brussels Sprouts!

These Truffle Roasted Brussels Sprouts are perfect for serving alongside roasted meats, poultry, or seafood. They make a delicious and elegant addition to any meal, and the luxurious aroma of truffles adds a special touch to the dish. Feel free to customize the recipe by adding other seasonings or toppings according to your taste preferences.

Truffle Cauliflower Gratin

Ingredients:

- 1 large head of cauliflower, cut into florets
- 2 tablespoons butter
- 2 tablespoons all-purpose flour
- 1 1/2 cups milk
- 1/2 cup grated Parmesan cheese
- 1/4 cup grated Gruyere cheese
- 2 tablespoons truffle oil
- 2 cloves garlic, minced
- Salt and pepper to taste
- Bread crumbs (optional, for topping)
- Chopped fresh parsley for garnish (optional)

Instructions:

Preheat your oven to 375°F (190°C). Grease a baking dish with butter or non-stick cooking spray.

Bring a large pot of salted water to a boil. Add the cauliflower florets and cook for 5 minutes, or until they are just tender. Drain the cauliflower and set aside.

In a medium saucepan, melt the butter over medium heat. Add the minced garlic and cook for 1-2 minutes, until fragrant.

Stir in the flour and cook for an additional 1-2 minutes, stirring constantly, until the mixture is smooth and bubbly.

Gradually whisk in the milk, stirring constantly, until the mixture is thickened and smooth.

Remove the saucepan from the heat and stir in the grated Parmesan cheese, grated Gruyere cheese, and truffle oil. Season with salt and pepper to taste.

Place the cooked cauliflower florets in the prepared baking dish. Pour the cheese sauce evenly over the cauliflower.

If desired, sprinkle bread crumbs over the top of the cauliflower gratin for added crunch and texture.

Bake the Truffle Cauliflower Gratin in the preheated oven for 25-30 minutes, or until the top is golden brown and bubbly.

Remove the gratin from the oven and let it cool for a few minutes before serving.

Garnish with chopped fresh parsley before serving, if desired.

Serve the Truffle Cauliflower Gratin hot as a delicious and indulgent side dish.

Enjoy the rich and flavorful taste of this Truffle Cauliflower Gratin!

This Truffle Cauliflower Gratin is perfect for serving alongside roasted meats, poultry, or seafood. It's a creamy and decadent dish that will impress your family and guests with its luxurious flavor. Feel free to customize the recipe by adding other cheeses or seasonings according to your taste preferences.

Truffle Creamed Spinach

Ingredients:

- 1 lb (450g) fresh spinach, washed and trimmed
- 2 tablespoons butter
- 2 cloves garlic, minced
- 2 tablespoons all-purpose flour
- 1 cup heavy cream
- 1/4 cup grated Parmesan cheese
- 1 tablespoon truffle oil
- Salt and pepper to taste
- Pinch of nutmeg (optional)

Instructions:

In a large skillet or saucepan, melt the butter over medium heat. Add the minced garlic and cook for 1-2 minutes, until fragrant.
Add the fresh spinach to the skillet and cook, stirring occasionally, until wilted and tender, about 3-5 minutes. Remove the spinach from the skillet and set aside.
In the same skillet, add the flour and cook, stirring constantly, for 1-2 minutes to make a roux.
Gradually whisk in the heavy cream, stirring constantly, until the mixture is smooth and thickened.
Stir in the grated Parmesan cheese until melted and well combined.
Add the truffle oil to the cream sauce and stir to incorporate. Season with salt, pepper, and a pinch of nutmeg, if using, to taste.
Return the cooked spinach to the skillet and toss to coat it evenly with the cream sauce.
Cook the Truffle Creamed Spinach for an additional 2-3 minutes, until heated through.
Once done, remove the skillet from the heat.
Serve the Truffle Creamed Spinach hot as a delicious and indulgent side dish.
Enjoy the rich and flavorful taste of this Truffle Creamed Spinach!

This Truffle Creamed Spinach is perfect for serving alongside roasted meats, poultry, or seafood. It's creamy, savory, and packed with the luxurious aroma of truffles. Feel free to adjust the amount of truffle oil according to your taste preferences, and garnish with additional grated Parmesan cheese if desired.

Truffle Polenta Fries

Ingredients:

- 1 cup polenta (coarse cornmeal)
- 4 cups water
- 1 teaspoon salt
- 2 tablespoons butter
- 1/4 cup grated Parmesan cheese
- 2 tablespoons truffle oil
- Salt and pepper to taste
- Vegetable oil, for frying

Instructions:

In a medium saucepan, bring the water to a boil. Add the salt.
Gradually whisk in the polenta, stirring constantly to prevent lumps from forming.
Reduce the heat to low and simmer the polenta, stirring frequently, until it is thick and creamy, about 20-30 minutes.
Once the polenta is cooked, remove it from the heat and stir in the butter, grated Parmesan cheese, and truffle oil. Season with salt and pepper to taste.
Spread the cooked polenta evenly in a shallow baking dish or pan lined with parchment paper. Smooth the top with a spatula.
Refrigerate the polenta for at least 1 hour, or until it is firm and set.
Once the polenta is chilled and firm, remove it from the refrigerator and cut it into thick fries or wedges.
Heat vegetable oil in a deep fryer or large skillet to 350°F (175°C).
Fry the polenta fries in batches until they are golden brown and crispy, about 3-4 minutes per batch.
Remove the fried polenta fries from the oil and drain them on paper towels.
Season the Truffle Polenta Fries with additional salt and pepper, if desired.
Serve the Truffle Polenta Fries hot as a delicious and indulgent appetizer or side dish.
Enjoy the rich and flavorful taste of these Truffle Polenta Fries!

These Truffle Polenta Fries are crispy on the outside and creamy on the inside, with the irresistible aroma of truffles. They're perfect for serving with your favorite dipping sauce, such as aioli or marinara sauce. Feel free to customize the recipe by adding additional seasonings or herbs to the polenta mixture before chilling.

Truffle Tuna Tartare

Ingredients:

- 8 oz (225g) sushi-grade tuna, diced into small cubes
- 1 tablespoon truffle oil
- 1 tablespoon soy sauce
- 1 teaspoon sesame oil
- 1 teaspoon grated fresh ginger
- 1 teaspoon minced garlic
- 1 green onion, finely chopped
- 1 tablespoon chopped fresh cilantro
- 1 teaspoon toasted sesame seeds
- Salt and pepper to taste
- Optional: thinly sliced radishes or cucumber, for serving
- Optional: microgreens or edible flowers, for garnish

Instructions:

In a mixing bowl, combine the diced tuna, truffle oil, soy sauce, sesame oil, grated ginger, minced garlic, chopped green onion, chopped cilantro, and toasted sesame seeds. Mix gently to combine.
Season the Truffle Tuna Tartare mixture with salt and pepper to taste. Adjust the seasoning as needed.
Cover the bowl with plastic wrap and refrigerate the tuna tartare for at least 30 minutes to allow the flavors to meld together.
Once chilled, remove the tuna tartare from the refrigerator and taste it again, adjusting the seasoning if necessary.
To serve, divide the Truffle Tuna Tartare mixture among individual serving dishes or onto a platter.
If desired, garnish the tuna tartare with thinly sliced radishes or cucumber, and top with microgreens or edible flowers for an elegant touch.
Serve the Truffle Tuna Tartare immediately as a sophisticated appetizer, accompanied by crispy wonton chips, crackers, or toasted baguette slices.
Enjoy the fresh and flavorful taste of this Truffle Tuna Tartare!

This Truffle Tuna Tartare is perfect for serving at dinner parties, special occasions, or as an elegant appetizer for a romantic dinner. The combination of fresh tuna and truffle oil creates a dish that is both luxurious and delicious. Feel free to customize the recipe by adding additional ingredients such as avocado, mango, or cucumber for extra flavor and texture.

Truffle Crab Cakes

Ingredients:

- 1 lb (450g) lump crab meat, drained
- 1/2 cup breadcrumbs
- 1/4 cup mayonnaise
- 1 large egg, beaten
- 1 tablespoon Dijon mustard
- 2 tablespoons chopped fresh parsley
- 1 tablespoon truffle oil
- 1 teaspoon Old Bay seasoning
- Salt and pepper to taste
- Vegetable oil, for frying
- Lemon wedges, for serving
- Optional: tartar sauce or aioli, for serving

Instructions:

In a large mixing bowl, combine the lump crab meat, breadcrumbs, mayonnaise, beaten egg, Dijon mustard, chopped parsley, truffle oil, Old Bay seasoning, salt, and pepper. Gently mix until all ingredients are well combined.

Divide the crab mixture into equal portions and shape each portion into a small patty or cake. Place the crab cakes on a baking sheet lined with parchment paper and refrigerate for at least 30 minutes to firm up.

Heat vegetable oil in a large skillet over medium-high heat. Once the oil is hot, carefully add the crab cakes to the skillet in batches, being careful not to overcrowd the pan.

Fry the crab cakes for 3-4 minutes per side, or until golden brown and crispy. Use a spatula to carefully flip the crab cakes halfway through cooking.

Once the crab cakes are cooked through and golden brown on both sides, remove them from the skillet and transfer them to a plate lined with paper towels to drain any excess oil.

Serve the Truffle Crab Cakes hot, garnished with chopped parsley and lemon wedges on the side for squeezing over the crab cakes.

Optionally, serve the crab cakes with tartar sauce or aioli for dipping.

Enjoy the rich and delicious flavor of these Truffle Crab Cakes as an appetizer or main dish!

These Truffle Crab Cakes are perfect for serving at dinner parties, special occasions, or as an elegant appetizer for a romantic dinner. The addition of truffle oil adds a luxurious touch to the classic crab cake recipe, elevating it to a whole new level of flavor. Feel free to adjust the seasonings and spices to suit your taste preferences.

Truffle Shrimp Scampi

Ingredients:

- 1 lb (450g) large shrimp, peeled and deveined
- 4 tablespoons butter
- 4 cloves garlic, minced
- 1/4 cup white wine
- 2 tablespoons lemon juice
- 1 tablespoon truffle oil
- Salt and pepper to taste
- 2 tablespoons chopped fresh parsley
- Cooked pasta or crusty bread, for serving

Instructions:

Heat 2 tablespoons of butter in a large skillet over medium heat. Add the minced garlic and cook for 1-2 minutes, until fragrant.
Add the shrimp to the skillet and cook for 2-3 minutes on each side, until they turn pink and opaque. Remove the shrimp from the skillet and set aside.
In the same skillet, add the remaining 2 tablespoons of butter, white wine, and lemon juice. Bring the mixture to a simmer and let it cook for 2-3 minutes, until slightly reduced.
Stir in the truffle oil and season the sauce with salt and pepper to taste.
Return the cooked shrimp to the skillet and toss them in the truffle sauce until they are evenly coated.
Cook the Truffle Shrimp Scampi for an additional minute or two, until the shrimp are heated through.
Remove the skillet from the heat and garnish the Truffle Shrimp Scampi with chopped fresh parsley.
Serve the Truffle Shrimp Scampi hot, over cooked pasta or with crusty bread on the side.
Enjoy the rich and flavorful taste of this Truffle Shrimp Scampi!

This Truffle Shrimp Scampi is perfect for serving as a main dish for a special dinner or as an elegant appetizer for entertaining guests. The addition of truffle oil adds a luxurious touch to the classic shrimp scampi recipe, enhancing its flavor and aroma.

Feel free to adjust the amount of truffle oil according to your taste preferences, and serve the dish with your favorite pasta or bread for a complete and delicious meal.

Truffle Stuffed Chicken Breast

Ingredients:

- 2 boneless, skinless chicken breasts
- Salt and pepper to taste
- 2 tablespoons truffle oil
- 4 ounces (115g) cream cheese, softened
- 2 tablespoons grated Parmesan cheese
- 1 tablespoon chopped fresh parsley
- 1 clove garlic, minced
- 1/4 cup breadcrumbs
- 1 tablespoon butter, melted
- Optional: additional chopped fresh parsley for garnish

Instructions:

Preheat your oven to 375°F (190°C).

Place the chicken breasts on a cutting board and use a sharp knife to carefully butterfly each one, cutting horizontally through the thickest part of the breast, but not all the way through, so that you can open it like a book.

Season the inside of each butterflied chicken breast with salt and pepper to taste.

In a small bowl, mix together the truffle oil, softened cream cheese, grated Parmesan cheese, chopped parsley, and minced garlic until well combined.

Spread half of the truffle cream cheese mixture evenly onto each butterflied chicken breast.

Close the chicken breasts to encase the filling, and secure them with toothpicks if necessary.

In another small bowl, combine the breadcrumbs and melted butter.

Carefully coat each stuffed chicken breast with the breadcrumb mixture, pressing gently to adhere.

Place the stuffed chicken breasts in a baking dish or on a baking sheet lined with parchment paper.

Bake the Truffle Stuffed Chicken Breast in the preheated oven for 25-30 minutes, or until the chicken is cooked through and the breadcrumbs are golden brown and crispy.

Once done, remove the stuffed chicken breasts from the oven and let them rest for a few minutes before serving.

Garnish the Truffle Stuffed Chicken Breast with additional chopped fresh parsley, if desired.
Serve the stuffed chicken breasts hot as a delicious and elegant main dish.
Enjoy the rich and flavorful taste of this Truffle Stuffed Chicken Breast!

This Truffle Stuffed Chicken Breast is perfect for serving at dinner parties, special occasions, or as a gourmet meal for a romantic dinner. The creamy truffle filling adds a luxurious touch to the tender chicken breast, making it a dish that is sure to impress. Feel free to customize the recipe by adding additional herbs or spices to the filling according to your taste preferences.

Truffle Quiche

Ingredients:

For the Pastry Crust:

- 1 1/4 cups all-purpose flour
- 1/2 teaspoon salt
- 1/2 cup unsalted butter, cold and cut into small cubes
- 2-3 tablespoons ice water

For the Filling:

- 4 large eggs
- 1 cup heavy cream
- 1/2 cup milk
- 1/2 cup grated Gruyere cheese
- 1/4 cup grated Parmesan cheese
- 1 tablespoon truffle oil
- Salt and pepper to taste
- 1/4 cup chopped fresh parsley
- Optional: sliced mushrooms, caramelized onions, cooked bacon, or spinach

Instructions:

Preheat your oven to 375°F (190°C).
In a food processor, combine the all-purpose flour and salt. Add the cold butter cubes and pulse until the mixture resembles coarse crumbs.
Gradually add the ice water, 1 tablespoon at a time, and pulse until the dough comes together and forms a ball.
Transfer the dough to a lightly floured surface and roll it out into a circle large enough to fit your quiche pan or pie dish.
Carefully transfer the rolled-out dough to the quiche pan or pie dish. Press the dough into the bottom and up the sides of the pan. Trim off any excess dough.
Prick the bottom of the pastry crust with a fork and bake it in the preheated oven for 10-12 minutes, or until it is set and lightly golden brown. Remove from the oven and let it cool slightly.

In a mixing bowl, whisk together the eggs, heavy cream, and milk until well combined. Stir in the grated Gruyere cheese, grated Parmesan cheese, truffle oil, salt, pepper, and chopped parsley.

If desired, add any optional ingredients such as sliced mushrooms, caramelized onions, cooked bacon, or spinach to the filling mixture.

Pour the filling mixture into the partially baked pastry crust.

Return the quiche to the oven and bake for 30-35 minutes, or until the filling is set and the top is golden brown.

Once done, remove the Truffle Quiche from the oven and let it cool for a few minutes before slicing and serving.

Serve the Truffle Quiche warm or at room temperature as a delicious and satisfying meal.

Enjoy the rich and flavorful taste of this Truffle Quiche!

This Truffle Quiche is perfect for brunch, lunch, or a light dinner. The combination of creamy eggs, cheese, and truffle oil creates a decadent and satisfying dish that is sure to impress. Feel free to customize the filling with your favorite ingredients or add extra herbs and spices for added flavor.

Truffle Gnocchi

Ingredients:

For the Gnocchi:

- 2 large russet potatoes (about 1 pound each)
- 1 egg, beaten
- 1 1/2 cups all-purpose flour, plus more for dusting
- Salt to taste
- 1 tablespoon truffle oil

For the Truffle Sauce:

- 4 tablespoons unsalted butter
- 2 cloves garlic, minced
- 1 tablespoon truffle oil
- Salt and pepper to taste
- Grated Parmesan cheese for garnish
- Chopped fresh parsley for garnish

Instructions:

Preheat your oven to 400°F (200°C). Pierce the potatoes all over with a fork and place them on a baking sheet. Bake for 45-60 minutes, or until tender when pierced with a fork.
Remove the potatoes from the oven and let them cool slightly. Once cool enough to handle, peel off the skins and discard them.
In a large mixing bowl, mash the peeled potatoes until smooth using a potato masher or ricer. Let the mashed potatoes cool completely.
Once cooled, add the beaten egg, flour, salt, and truffle oil to the mashed potatoes. Mix until a soft dough forms.
Turn the dough out onto a lightly floured surface. Divide the dough into several portions and roll each portion into a long rope, about 1/2 inch in diameter.
Cut each rope into bite-sized pieces, about 1 inch long. Use a fork to create ridges on each gnocchi, if desired.

Bring a large pot of salted water to a boil. Working in batches, drop the gnocchi into the boiling water and cook until they float to the surface, about 2-3 minutes. Use a slotted spoon to transfer the cooked gnocchi to a plate lined with paper towels to drain.

In a large skillet, melt the butter over medium heat. Add the minced garlic and cook until fragrant, about 1 minute.

Add the cooked gnocchi to the skillet and drizzle with truffle oil. Toss gently to coat the gnocchi in the truffle butter sauce. Season with salt and pepper to taste.

Transfer the Truffle Gnocchi to serving plates. Garnish with grated Parmesan cheese and chopped fresh parsley.

Serve the Truffle Gnocchi immediately, while hot, as a delicious and indulgent main dish or side.

Enjoy the rich and luxurious taste of this Truffle Gnocchi!

This Truffle Gnocchi is perfect for a special dinner or celebration. The delicate potato dumplings combined with the aromatic truffle oil create a dish that is both comforting and elegant. Serve it alongside a simple salad or roasted vegetables for a complete meal.

Truffle Beef Wellington

Ingredients:

- 1 1/2 lbs (680g) beef tenderloin fillet, trimmed
- Salt and pepper to taste
- 2 tablespoons olive oil
- 1 tablespoon truffle oil
- 1/4 cup finely chopped mushrooms (such as button or cremini)
- 2 cloves garlic, minced
- 1 tablespoon finely chopped fresh thyme
- 2 tablespoons butter
- 4 slices prosciutto
- 1 sheet puff pastry, thawed if frozen
- 1 egg, beaten (for egg wash)

Instructions:

Preheat your oven to 425°F (220°C).

Season the beef tenderloin fillet generously with salt and pepper on all sides.

Heat the olive oil in a large skillet over high heat. Once hot, sear the beef fillet on all sides until browned, about 2 minutes per side. Remove the beef from the skillet and let it cool slightly.

In the same skillet, add the truffle oil, chopped mushrooms, minced garlic, and fresh thyme. Cook until the mushrooms are soft and the garlic is fragrant, about 3-4 minutes. Remove from heat and let it cool.

Spread the slices of prosciutto on a clean surface, slightly overlapping each other to form a rectangle large enough to wrap the beef fillet.

Spread the cooled mushroom mixture evenly over the prosciutto slices.

Place the seared beef fillet in the center of the mushroom-covered prosciutto slices. Carefully roll the prosciutto and mushrooms around the beef to encase it completely.

Roll out the puff pastry on a lightly floured surface into a rectangle large enough to wrap the beef fillet completely.

Place the wrapped beef fillet seam side down on the puff pastry. Fold the puff pastry over the beef, trimming any excess pastry if necessary. Seal the edges by pressing them together gently.

Place the Truffle Beef Wellington seam side down on a baking sheet lined with parchment paper.

Brush the top and sides of the pastry with the beaten egg to create an egg wash. Using a sharp knife, score the top of the pastry lightly in a decorative pattern, being careful not to cut all the way through the pastry.

Bake the Truffle Beef Wellington in the preheated oven for 25-30 minutes, or until the pastry is golden brown and crisp, and the beef reaches your desired level of doneness (for medium-rare, aim for an internal temperature of about 135°F or 57°C).

Once done, remove the Truffle Beef Wellington from the oven and let it rest for 5-10 minutes before slicing.

Slice the Truffle Beef Wellington into thick slices and serve hot.

Enjoy the rich and luxurious taste of this Truffle Beef Wellington!

This Truffle Beef Wellington is perfect for a special occasion or holiday meal. Serve it with your favorite sides such as mashed potatoes and roasted vegetables for a truly decadent dining experience.

Truffle Ratatouille

Ingredients:

- 1 eggplant, diced
- 2 zucchini, diced
- 1 yellow bell pepper, diced
- 1 red bell pepper, diced
- 1 onion, diced
- 3 cloves garlic, minced
- 2 tablespoons olive oil
- 1 can (14 oz) diced tomatoes
- 1 tablespoon tomato paste
- 1 teaspoon dried thyme
- 1 teaspoon dried oregano
- Salt and pepper to taste
- 1 tablespoon truffle oil
- Chopped fresh basil for garnish

Instructions:

Heat the olive oil in a large skillet or pot over medium heat. Add the diced onion and garlic, and cook until softened and fragrant, about 5 minutes.

Add the diced eggplant, zucchini, and bell peppers to the skillet. Cook, stirring occasionally, until the vegetables are tender, about 10 minutes.

Stir in the diced tomatoes, tomato paste, dried thyme, dried oregano, salt, and pepper. Simmer the ratatouille mixture for an additional 10-15 minutes, until the flavors are well combined and the vegetables are cooked through.

Remove the skillet from the heat and drizzle the truffle oil over the ratatouille. Stir gently to incorporate the truffle oil into the mixture.

Taste and adjust the seasoning as needed, adding more salt and pepper if desired.

Transfer the Truffle Ratatouille to a serving dish and garnish with chopped fresh basil.

Serve the Truffle Ratatouille hot as a delicious and aromatic side dish or main course.

Enjoy the rich and flavorful taste of this Truffle Ratatouille!

This Truffle Ratatouille is perfect for serving alongside grilled meats, poultry, or fish, or as a vegetarian main dish served over cooked grains or pasta. The addition of truffle oil adds a luxurious touch to the classic ratatouille recipe, elevating it to a whole new level of flavor. Feel free to customize the recipe by adding other vegetables such as mushrooms, carrots, or celery according to your taste preferences.

Truffle Eggplant Parmesan

Ingredients:

- 2 medium eggplants, sliced into 1/2-inch rounds
- Salt
- 1 cup all-purpose flour
- 2 large eggs, beaten
- 1 cup breadcrumbs
- 1/2 cup grated Parmesan cheese
- 2 cups marinara sauce
- 8 oz fresh mozzarella cheese, sliced
- 2 tablespoons truffle oil
- Fresh basil leaves, for garnish
- Optional: additional grated Parmesan cheese for serving

Instructions:

Preheat your oven to 375°F (190°C). Grease a baking sheet or line it with parchment paper.

Place the eggplant slices in a colander and sprinkle them generously with salt. Let them sit for about 30 minutes to release excess moisture. Pat the eggplant slices dry with paper towels.

Set up a breading station with three shallow bowls: one with flour, one with beaten eggs, and one with breadcrumbs mixed with grated Parmesan cheese. Dredge each eggplant slice in the flour, shaking off any excess. Dip it into the beaten eggs, allowing any excess to drip off, then coat it in the breadcrumb mixture. Place the breaded eggplant slices on the prepared baking sheet in a single layer.

Bake the breaded eggplant slices in the preheated oven for about 15-20 minutes, or until they are golden brown and crispy. Remove them from the oven and set aside.

In a baking dish, spread a thin layer of marinara sauce on the bottom. Arrange a layer of baked eggplant slices on top of the sauce.

Drizzle a little truffle oil over the eggplant slices, then spoon more marinara sauce on top. Add slices of fresh mozzarella cheese on top of the sauce.

Repeat the layers until all the ingredients are used, finishing with a layer of marinara sauce and mozzarella cheese on top.

Drizzle a little more truffle oil over the top layer of cheese.

Bake the Truffle Eggplant Parmesan in the preheated oven for about 25-30 minutes, or until the cheese is melted and bubbly and the edges are golden brown.

Remove the baking dish from the oven and let the Truffle Eggplant Parmesan cool for a few minutes before serving.

Garnish with fresh basil leaves and additional grated Parmesan cheese, if desired.

Serve the Truffle Eggplant Parmesan hot as a delicious and indulgent main dish. Enjoy the rich and flavorful taste of this Truffle Eggplant Parmesan!

This Truffle Eggplant Parmesan is perfect for serving as a comforting and satisfying meal for family dinners or special occasions. The addition of truffle oil adds a luxurious touch to the classic eggplant parmesan recipe, elevating it to a whole new level of flavor. Feel free to adjust the amount of truffle oil according to your taste preferences.

Truffle Lamb Chops

Ingredients:

- 4 lamb chops, about 1 inch thick
- Salt and pepper to taste
- 2 tablespoons olive oil
- 2 cloves garlic, minced
- 1 tablespoon chopped fresh rosemary
- 1 tablespoon truffle oil
- Optional: chopped fresh parsley for garnish

Instructions:

Preheat your oven to 400°F (200°C).
Season the lamb chops generously with salt and pepper on both sides.
Heat the olive oil in a large skillet over medium-high heat. Add the minced garlic and chopped rosemary to the skillet and cook for 1-2 minutes, until fragrant.
Add the lamb chops to the skillet and sear them for 2-3 minutes on each side, until they are browned.
Transfer the seared lamb chops to a baking dish or oven-safe skillet.
Drizzle the truffle oil over the lamb chops, spreading it evenly with a brush or spoon.
Place the baking dish or skillet in the preheated oven and roast the lamb chops for 10-15 minutes, or until they reach your desired level of doneness. For medium-rare, aim for an internal temperature of about 145°F (63°C).
Once done, remove the Truffle Lamb Chops from the oven and let them rest for a few minutes before serving.
Garnish the Truffle Lamb Chops with chopped fresh parsley, if desired.
Serve the Truffle Lamb Chops hot as a delicious and indulgent main dish.
Enjoy the rich and flavorful taste of these Truffle Lamb Chops!

These Truffle Lamb Chops are perfect for serving as a special dinner entree for a romantic meal or dinner party. The addition of truffle oil adds a luxurious and elegant touch to the classic lamb chops, elevating them to a whole new level of flavor. Feel free to adjust the seasonings and herbs according to your taste preferences.

Truffle Paella

Ingredients:

- 2 cups Arborio rice
- 4 cups chicken or seafood broth
- 1 pinch saffron threads
- 1 onion, finely chopped
- 4 cloves garlic, minced
- 1 red bell pepper, diced
- 1 yellow bell pepper, diced
- 1 cup frozen peas
- 1 cup sliced mushrooms
- 1 cup cherry tomatoes, halved
- 1/2 cup white wine
- 1/4 cup truffle oil
- Salt and pepper to taste
- 1 lb assorted seafood (such as shrimp, mussels, and squid), cleaned and peeled
- Fresh parsley, chopped, for garnish
- Lemon wedges, for serving

Instructions:

In a small bowl, combine the saffron threads with 1/4 cup of warm broth. Let it sit and infuse for about 10-15 minutes.

In a large paella pan or skillet, heat the truffle oil over medium heat. Add the chopped onion and cook until softened, about 5 minutes.

Stir in the minced garlic and diced bell peppers, and cook for another 2-3 minutes until fragrant.

Add the Arborio rice to the pan and stir to coat the grains with the truffle oil and vegetables.

Pour in the white wine and cook until it is absorbed by the rice, stirring constantly.

Add the saffron-infused broth to the pan, along with the remaining chicken or seafood broth. Bring the mixture to a simmer.

Season the broth with salt and pepper to taste.

Arrange the assorted seafood, sliced mushrooms, cherry tomatoes, and frozen peas evenly over the rice mixture in the pan.

Cover the pan with a lid or aluminum foil and let the paella simmer gently for about 20-25 minutes, or until the rice is cooked and the seafood is cooked through.
Once done, remove the lid and let the paella rest for a few minutes before serving.
Garnish the Truffle Paella with chopped fresh parsley and serve hot with lemon wedges on the side.
Enjoy the rich and aromatic flavors of this Truffle Paella!

This Truffle Paella is perfect for serving as a main dish for a special occasion or dinner party. The addition of truffle oil adds a luxurious and elegant touch to the classic Spanish dish, elevating it to a whole new level of flavor. Feel free to customize the seafood and vegetables according to your taste preferences.

Truffle Vegetable Stir-fry

Ingredients:

- 2 tablespoons truffle oil
- 1 onion, thinly sliced
- 2 cloves garlic, minced
- 1 red bell pepper, thinly sliced
- 1 yellow bell pepper, thinly sliced
- 1 cup sliced mushrooms (such as button or cremini)
- 1 cup broccoli florets
- 1 cup snow peas, trimmed
- 1 carrot, julienned
- 1/4 cup vegetable broth or water
- 2 tablespoons soy sauce
- 1 tablespoon rice vinegar
- 1 tablespoon honey or brown sugar
- 1 teaspoon cornstarch mixed with 1 tablespoon water (optional, for thickening)
- Salt and pepper to taste
- Cooked rice or noodles, for serving
- Sesame seeds and chopped green onions for garnish (optional)

Instructions:

Heat the truffle oil in a large skillet or wok over medium-high heat.
Add the sliced onion and minced garlic to the skillet and stir-fry for 2-3 minutes, until fragrant and softened.
Add the sliced bell peppers, mushrooms, broccoli florets, snow peas, and julienned carrot to the skillet. Stir-fry for another 4-5 minutes, or until the vegetables are tender-crisp.
In a small bowl, whisk together the vegetable broth (or water), soy sauce, rice vinegar, and honey (or brown sugar) to make the sauce.
Pour the sauce over the vegetables in the skillet and toss to coat evenly. Cook for an additional 2-3 minutes, allowing the sauce to thicken slightly.
If desired, add the cornstarch-water mixture to the skillet to further thicken the sauce. Stir well and cook for another minute.
Season the Truffle Vegetable Stir-fry with salt and pepper to taste.

Remove the skillet from the heat and serve the Truffle Vegetable Stir-fry hot over cooked rice or noodles.
Garnish with sesame seeds and chopped green onions, if desired.
Enjoy the flavorful and aromatic taste of this Truffle Vegetable Stir-fry!

This Truffle Vegetable Stir-fry is perfect for a quick and healthy weeknight meal. The addition of truffle oil adds a luxurious and elegant touch to the classic stir-fry recipe, elevating it to a whole new level of flavor. Feel free to customize the vegetables and adjust the seasonings according to your taste preferences.

Truffle Beef Stroganoff

Ingredients:

- 1 lb (450g) beef tenderloin or sirloin steak, thinly sliced
- Salt and pepper to taste
- 2 tablespoons olive oil
- 1 onion, finely chopped
- 2 cloves garlic, minced
- 8 oz (225g) mushrooms, sliced
- 2 tablespoons all-purpose flour
- 1 cup beef broth
- 1 cup sour cream
- 2 tablespoons truffle oil
- 1 tablespoon Worcestershire sauce
- 1 teaspoon Dijon mustard
- 1/4 cup chopped fresh parsley, plus more for garnish
- Cooked egg noodles or rice, for serving

Instructions:

Season the thinly sliced beef strips with salt and pepper to taste.
Heat 1 tablespoon of olive oil in a large skillet over medium-high heat. Add the beef strips and cook them for 2-3 minutes per side, or until browned. Remove the beef from the skillet and set it aside on a plate.
In the same skillet, heat the remaining tablespoon of olive oil over medium heat. Add the chopped onion and minced garlic, and sauté them until softened and fragrant, about 2-3 minutes.
Add the sliced mushrooms to the skillet and cook them for 5-6 minutes, or until they are golden brown and tender.
Sprinkle the flour over the mushrooms and stir to coat them evenly. Cook for an additional 1-2 minutes to remove the raw flour taste.
Gradually pour in the beef broth, stirring constantly to prevent lumps from forming. Cook the mixture until it thickens slightly, about 2-3 minutes.
Reduce the heat to low and stir in the sour cream, truffle oil, Worcestershire sauce, and Dijon mustard. Cook for another 2-3 minutes, or until the sauce is heated through and well combined.

Return the cooked beef strips to the skillet and stir them into the sauce. Cook for an additional 2-3 minutes to heat the beef through.

Stir in the chopped fresh parsley, reserving some for garnish.

Remove the skillet from the heat and serve the Truffle Beef Stroganoff hot over cooked egg noodles or rice.

Garnish with additional chopped parsley before serving.

Enjoy the rich and decadent flavor of this Truffle Beef Stroganoff!

This Truffle Beef Stroganoff is perfect for serving as a comforting and satisfying meal for a cozy dinner at home. The addition of truffle oil adds a luxurious and elegant touch to the classic stroganoff recipe, elevating it to a whole new level of flavor. Feel free to customize the dish by adding your favorite herbs or vegetables according to your taste preferences.

Truffle Saffron Risotto

Ingredients:

- 1 cup Arborio rice
- 4 cups chicken or vegetable broth
- 1/4 teaspoon saffron threads
- 2 tablespoons truffle oil
- 1 tablespoon unsalted butter
- 1 small onion, finely chopped
- 2 cloves garlic, minced
- 1/2 cup dry white wine
- 1/4 cup grated Parmesan cheese
- Salt and pepper to taste
- Chopped fresh parsley or chives for garnish (optional)

Instructions:

In a small bowl, combine the saffron threads with 2 tablespoons of warm water. Let it steep for about 10-15 minutes to release the flavor and color.

In a medium saucepan, heat the chicken or vegetable broth over medium heat until it simmers. Reduce the heat to low to keep it warm.

In a large skillet or saucepan, heat the truffle oil and butter over medium heat. Add the chopped onion and garlic, and sauté until softened, about 2-3 minutes.

Add the Arborio rice to the skillet and stir to coat the grains with the truffle oil and onions. Cook for another 2-3 minutes, until the rice is lightly toasted.

Pour in the dry white wine and cook until it is absorbed by the rice, stirring constantly.

Begin adding the warm broth to the skillet, one ladleful at a time, stirring frequently. Allow each addition of broth to be absorbed by the rice before adding more. Continue this process until the rice is creamy and cooked al dente, about 18-20 minutes.

Stir in the steeped saffron threads along with the liquid into the risotto, making sure to evenly distribute the saffron throughout the dish.

Once the risotto is creamy and the rice is cooked, remove the skillet from the heat.

Stir in the grated Parmesan cheese until it is melted and fully incorporated into the risotto. Season with salt and pepper to taste.

Serve the Truffle Saffron Risotto hot, garnished with chopped fresh parsley or chives if desired.
Enjoy the rich and aromatic flavors of this Truffle Saffron Risotto!

This Truffle Saffron Risotto is perfect as a decadent side dish or a vegetarian main course for a special occasion or romantic dinner. The combination of saffron and truffle oil adds a luxurious and elegant touch to the creamy risotto, making it a truly indulgent dish. Adjust the amount of truffle oil according to your taste preferences, and feel free to add additional ingredients such as mushrooms or peas for extra flavor and texture.

Truffle Corn Chowder

Ingredients:

- 4 cups fresh or frozen corn kernels
- 1 onion, diced
- 2 cloves garlic, minced
- 4 cups vegetable or chicken broth
- 1 cup heavy cream
- 2 tablespoons truffle oil
- Salt and pepper to taste
- Chopped fresh parsley for garnish

Instructions:

Sauté Onion and Garlic: In a large pot, heat some olive oil over medium heat. Add diced onion and minced garlic. Sauté until the onion becomes translucent and fragrant, about 5 minutes.

Add Corn: Add the corn kernels to the pot and cook for another 5 minutes, stirring occasionally.

Simmer: Pour in the vegetable or chicken broth. Bring the mixture to a boil, then reduce the heat and let it simmer for about 15-20 minutes, allowing the flavors to meld together.

Blend: Using an immersion blender or transferring the mixture to a blender in batches, blend the soup until smooth. Be careful when blending hot liquids.

Add Cream and Truffle Oil: Return the soup to the pot if necessary and stir in the heavy cream and truffle oil. Season with salt and pepper to taste. Let it simmer for an additional 5 minutes to heat through and allow the flavors to blend.

Serve: Ladle the truffle corn chowder into bowls and garnish with chopped fresh parsley. Optionally, drizzle a little extra truffle oil on top for added flavor.

Enjoy: Serve the chowder hot and enjoy its rich, comforting flavors.

This recipe is quite versatile, so feel free to adjust the quantities of ingredients according to your taste preferences. You can also add other ingredients like diced potatoes or crispy bacon for extra texture and flavor.

Truffle Potato Gratin

Ingredients:

- 2 pounds Yukon Gold potatoes, peeled and thinly sliced
- 2 cups heavy cream
- 2 cloves garlic, minced
- 1 cup grated Gruyere cheese (or any other melting cheese of your choice)
- 2 tablespoons truffle oil
- Salt and pepper to taste
- Chopped fresh chives or parsley for garnish (optional)

Instructions:

Preheat Oven: Preheat your oven to 375°F (190°C). Grease a baking dish with butter or cooking spray.
Layer Potatoes: Arrange a layer of thinly sliced potatoes in the bottom of the baking dish, overlapping them slightly.
Prepare Cream Mixture: In a saucepan, heat the heavy cream and minced garlic over medium heat until it just starts to simmer. Remove from heat and let it cool slightly.
Add Cheese and Truffle Oil: Stir the grated Gruyere cheese into the warm cream mixture until it's melted and well combined. Then, stir in the truffle oil. Season the mixture with salt and pepper to taste.
Layer and Repeat: Pour a portion of the cream mixture over the layer of potatoes in the baking dish, ensuring they are evenly coated. Repeat layering potatoes and cream mixture until all the potatoes and cream mixture are used, ending with a layer of cream on top.
Cover and Bake: Cover the baking dish with aluminum foil and bake in the preheated oven for about 45 minutes, or until the potatoes are tender when pierced with a knife.
Uncover and Finish: Remove the foil and continue baking for an additional 15-20 minutes, or until the top is golden brown and bubbly.
Garnish and Serve: Once cooked, remove the gratin from the oven and let it cool for a few minutes. Garnish with chopped fresh chives or parsley, if desired, before serving.
Serve: Serve the truffle potato gratin as a delicious side dish alongside your favorite main course.

This dish is perfect for special occasions or whenever you want to impress your guests with a decadent and flavorful potato dish. Enjoy!

Truffle Baked Brie

Ingredients:

- 1 wheel of brie cheese (about 8-10 ounces)
- 2 tablespoons truffle oil
- 2 tablespoons honey
- 1/4 cup chopped nuts (such as almonds, walnuts, or pecans)
- Sliced baguette, crackers, or apple slices for serving

Instructions:

Preheat Oven: Preheat your oven to 350°F (175°C).
Prepare Brie: Remove any packaging from the brie cheese and place it on a baking sheet lined with parchment paper or aluminum foil.
Drizzle with Truffle Oil: Drizzle the truffle oil over the top of the brie cheese, ensuring it covers the surface evenly.
Add Honey: Drizzle the honey over the truffle oil-covered brie cheese.
Sprinkle Nuts: Sprinkle the chopped nuts over the top of the brie cheese, pressing them gently into the surface to adhere.
Bake: Place the baking sheet with the brie cheese in the preheated oven and bake for 10-15 minutes, or until the cheese is soft and gooey inside and the nuts are lightly toasted.
Serve: Once baked, carefully transfer the baked brie to a serving platter. Surround it with sliced baguette, crackers, or apple slices for serving.
Enjoy: Serve the truffle baked brie immediately while it's warm and gooey. Allow your guests to scoop out portions of the melted cheese onto their bread or crackers.

This truffle baked brie makes for an elegant and delicious appetizer for parties, gatherings, or special occasions. The combination of creamy brie, earthy truffle oil, sweet honey, and crunchy nuts is sure to impress your guests. Enjoy!

Truffle Tomato Bruschetta

Ingredients:

- 4 ripe tomatoes, diced
- 2 cloves garlic, minced
- 2 tablespoons extra virgin olive oil
- 1 tablespoon truffle oil
- 1 tablespoon balsamic vinegar
- Salt and pepper to taste
- Fresh basil leaves, thinly sliced
- 1 baguette, sliced into rounds
- Optional: Grated Parmesan cheese for topping

Instructions:

Prepare Tomatoes: In a mixing bowl, combine the diced tomatoes, minced garlic, extra virgin olive oil, truffle oil, balsamic vinegar, salt, and pepper. Stir gently to combine, making sure the tomatoes are evenly coated. Allow the mixture to marinate for at least 15-20 minutes to let the flavors meld together.

Toast Baguette Slices: Preheat your oven to 375°F (190°C). Arrange the baguette slices on a baking sheet in a single layer. Toast them in the preheated oven for about 5-7 minutes, or until they are lightly golden and crispy.

Assemble Bruschetta: Once the baguette slices are toasted, remove them from the oven and allow them to cool slightly. Spoon a generous amount of the marinated tomato mixture onto each toasted baguette slice.

Garnish: Sprinkle some thinly sliced fresh basil leaves on top of each bruschetta.

Optional Topping: If desired, sprinkle a little grated Parmesan cheese over the top of each bruschetta for added flavor.

Serve: Arrange the truffle tomato bruschetta on a serving platter and serve immediately, while the baguette slices are still warm and crispy.

Enjoy: Enjoy the delicious combination of ripe tomatoes, aromatic truffle oil, and fresh basil on crispy toasted bread. These bruschetta make for a perfect appetizer or light snack for any occasion.

Feel free to adjust the quantities of ingredients according to your taste preferences. You can also add other ingredients like chopped onions or olives for additional flavor and texture.

Truffle Avocado Toast

Ingredients:

- 2 ripe avocados
- 4 slices of bread (sourdough or whole grain works well)
- 2 tablespoons truffle oil
- 1 tablespoon lemon juice
- Salt and pepper to taste
- Red pepper flakes (optional, for garnish)
- Fresh herbs (such as chives or parsley), thinly sliced for garnish

Instructions:

Prepare Avocado: Cut the avocados in half, remove the pits, and scoop the flesh into a bowl. Mash the avocado with a fork until it reaches your desired consistency (some prefer it smooth, while others like it chunky).
Season Avocado: Add the truffle oil, lemon juice, salt, and pepper to the mashed avocado. Stir until well combined. Taste and adjust seasoning if necessary.
Toast Bread: Toast the slices of bread until they are golden brown and crispy. You can use a toaster or toast them in a skillet with a little olive oil for extra flavor.
Assemble Avocado Toast: Spread a generous amount of the truffle avocado mixture onto each slice of toasted bread, spreading it evenly to the edges.
Garnish: Sprinkle a pinch of red pepper flakes over each avocado toast for a hint of spice, if desired. Then, garnish with thinly sliced fresh herbs for added freshness and color.
Serve: Arrange the truffle avocado toast on a serving plate and serve immediately while the toast is still warm and crispy.
Enjoy: Enjoy the delicious and decadent flavors of truffle-infused avocado on crispy toast. This makes for a perfect breakfast, brunch, or snack option that's both satisfying and full of flavor.

Feel free to customize your truffle avocado toast with additional toppings such as sliced tomatoes, poached eggs, or crumbled feta cheese for extra indulgence.

Truffle Caprese Salad

Ingredients:

- 2 large ripe tomatoes, sliced
- 1 ball of fresh mozzarella cheese, sliced
- Fresh basil leaves
- 2 tablespoons extra virgin olive oil
- 1 tablespoon truffle oil
- Balsamic glaze, for drizzling
- Salt and pepper to taste

Instructions:

Prepare Ingredients: Slice the tomatoes and mozzarella cheese into rounds of approximately the same thickness.
Assemble Salad: Arrange the tomato and mozzarella slices alternately on a serving platter, overlapping them slightly. Tuck fresh basil leaves in between the slices.
Drizzle Oils: In a small bowl, whisk together the extra virgin olive oil and truffle oil. Drizzle the oil mixture over the assembled salad.
Season: Sprinkle salt and pepper over the salad to taste.
Finish with Balsamic Glaze: Drizzle balsamic glaze over the top of the salad in a decorative pattern. If you don't have balsamic glaze, you can use balsamic vinegar instead, but reduce it in a saucepan over low heat until it thickens slightly.
Serve: Serve the Truffle Caprese Salad immediately, allowing the flavors to meld together.
Enjoy: Enjoy the combination of ripe tomatoes, creamy mozzarella, fragrant basil, and the earthy aroma of truffles in this elegant and flavorful salad.

This Truffle Caprese Salad is perfect as an appetizer, side dish, or light lunch. It's simple to make but impresses with its vibrant colors and delicious flavors.

Truffle Spinach and Artichoke Dip

Ingredients:

- 1 (10-ounce) package frozen chopped spinach, thawed and drained
- 1 (14-ounce) can artichoke hearts, drained and chopped
- 8 ounces cream cheese, softened
- 1/2 cup mayonnaise
- 1/2 cup sour cream
- 1 cup grated Parmesan cheese
- 2 cloves garlic, minced
- 2 tablespoons truffle oil
- Salt and pepper to taste
- Optional: Grated mozzarella cheese for topping

Instructions:

Preheat Oven: Preheat your oven to 375°F (190°C). Grease a baking dish with butter or cooking spray.
Mix Ingredients: In a large mixing bowl, combine the chopped spinach, chopped artichoke hearts, softened cream cheese, mayonnaise, sour cream, grated Parmesan cheese, minced garlic, and truffle oil. Mix until all ingredients are well combined.
Season: Season the mixture with salt and pepper to taste. Remember that the Parmesan cheese adds saltiness, so adjust accordingly.
Transfer to Baking Dish: Transfer the mixture to the prepared baking dish, spreading it out evenly.
Optional Topping: If desired, sprinkle some grated mozzarella cheese over the top of the dip for an extra cheesy crust.
Bake: Place the baking dish in the preheated oven and bake for about 25-30 minutes, or until the dip is hot and bubbly, and the cheese on top is melted and golden brown.
Serve: Once baked, remove the dip from the oven and let it cool slightly before serving.
Enjoy: Serve the truffle spinach and artichoke dip warm with tortilla chips, crackers, sliced baguette, or vegetable sticks for dipping.

This decadent and flavorful dip is sure to be a hit at any gathering or party. The addition of truffle oil adds a unique and sophisticated touch to the classic spinach and artichoke combination. Enjoy!

Truffle Pesto Pasta

Ingredients:

- 12 ounces (340g) pasta of your choice (such as spaghetti, fettuccine, or penne)
- 1 cup fresh basil leaves, packed
- 2 cloves garlic, peeled
- 1/4 cup pine nuts or walnuts
- 1/2 cup grated Parmesan cheese
- 1/4 cup extra virgin olive oil
- 2 tablespoons truffle oil
- Salt and pepper to taste
- Grated Parmesan cheese and chopped fresh basil for garnish (optional)

Instructions:

Cook Pasta: Cook the pasta according to the package instructions until it is al dente. Reserve about 1/2 cup of the pasta cooking water, then drain the pasta and set it aside.

Prepare Pesto: In a food processor, combine the fresh basil leaves, garlic cloves, pine nuts or walnuts, grated Parmesan cheese, and a pinch of salt and pepper. Pulse until the ingredients are finely chopped.

Add Oils: With the food processor running, slowly pour in the extra virgin olive oil and truffle oil until the mixture forms a smooth pesto sauce. If the pesto is too thick, you can thin it out with a little bit of the reserved pasta cooking water.

Toss Pasta: In a large skillet or saucepan, combine the cooked pasta and truffle pesto sauce. Toss the pasta gently until it is evenly coated with the sauce and heated through.

Adjust Seasoning: Taste the pasta and adjust the seasoning with salt and pepper if necessary.

Serve: Transfer the truffle pesto pasta to serving plates or a large serving bowl. Garnish with additional grated Parmesan cheese and chopped fresh basil, if desired.

Enjoy: Serve the truffle pesto pasta immediately while it's hot, and enjoy the wonderful combination of flavors and aromas.

This truffle pesto pasta is a luxurious and satisfying dish that's perfect for a special dinner or any time you're craving something indulgent. The truffle oil adds a delightful depth of flavor that elevates the classic pesto to new heights. Enjoy!

Truffle Chicken Piccata

Ingredients:

- 4 boneless, skinless chicken breasts
- Salt and pepper to taste
- All-purpose flour, for dredging
- 2 tablespoons olive oil
- 4 tablespoons unsalted butter, divided
- 1/2 cup chicken broth
- 1/4 cup fresh lemon juice (about 2 lemons)
- 1/4 cup brined capers, rinsed and drained
- 2 tablespoons truffle oil
- 2 tablespoons chopped fresh parsley, for garnish
- Lemon slices, for garnish (optional)

Instructions:

Prepare Chicken: Place the chicken breasts between two sheets of plastic wrap and gently pound them to an even thickness, about 1/2 inch. Season both sides of the chicken breasts with salt and pepper.
Dredge Chicken: Dredge the seasoned chicken breasts in flour, shaking off any excess.
Cook Chicken: In a large skillet, heat the olive oil and 2 tablespoons of butter over medium-high heat. Once the butter has melted and the skillet is hot, add the chicken breasts. Cook for about 4-5 minutes on each side, or until they are golden brown and cooked through. Transfer the cooked chicken breasts to a plate and cover them loosely with foil to keep warm.
Make Sauce: In the same skillet, add the chicken broth, lemon juice, and capers. Bring the mixture to a simmer, scraping up any browned bits from the bottom of the skillet. Let it cook for about 2-3 minutes, or until the sauce has slightly reduced and thickened.
Add Truffle Oil: Remove the skillet from the heat and stir in the truffle oil and remaining 2 tablespoons of butter until the butter has melted and the sauce is smooth and glossy.
Serve: Return the cooked chicken breasts to the skillet, turning them to coat evenly in the sauce. Garnish with chopped fresh parsley and lemon slices, if desired.
Enjoy: Serve the truffle chicken piccata immediately, accompanied by your favorite side dishes such as pasta, rice, or roasted vegetables.

This truffle-infused chicken piccata is sure to impress with its rich and tangy flavors. It's perfect for a special dinner at home or any time you're craving a gourmet meal. Enjoy!

Truffle Chocolate Fondue

Ingredients:

- 8 ounces (about 225g) dark chocolate, chopped
- 1/2 cup heavy cream
- 1 tablespoon truffle oil
- Assorted dipping ingredients (such as strawberries, bananas, marshmallows, pretzels, pound cake, etc.)

Instructions:

Prepare Chocolate: Place the chopped dark chocolate in a heatproof bowl.
Heat Cream: In a small saucepan, heat the heavy cream over medium heat until it just begins to simmer. Be careful not to let it boil.
Pour over Chocolate: Pour the hot cream over the chopped chocolate in the bowl. Let it sit for about 1 minute to soften the chocolate.
Stir: After 1 minute, begin stirring the chocolate and cream together until the chocolate is completely melted and the mixture is smooth and glossy.
Add Truffle Oil: Once the chocolate is smooth, stir in the truffle oil until it's well incorporated. The truffle oil will add a luxurious aroma to the fondue.
Transfer to Fondue Pot: Transfer the truffle chocolate fondue to a fondue pot or a heatproof serving bowl that can be placed over a small heat source.
Serve: Arrange the assorted dipping ingredients on a platter or in small bowls around the fondue pot.
Enjoy: Serve the truffle chocolate fondue immediately with the dipping ingredients. Use skewers or fondue forks to dip the items into the warm chocolate and enjoy the rich, indulgent flavors.

This truffle chocolate fondue is perfect for parties, romantic evenings, or any time you want to treat yourself to a special dessert experience. Experiment with different dipping ingredients to find your favorite combination!

www.ingramcontent.com/pod-product-compliance
Lightning Source LLC
LaVergne TN
LVHW081611060526
838201LV00054B/2207